The Official
Arsenal
Annual 2011

Written by Chas Newkey-Burden

A Grange Publication

™©(2010) The Arsenal Football Club plc. All rights reserved. Manufactured and distributed under licence by Grange Communications Ltd., Edinburgh. Printed in the EU.

Every effort has been made to ensure the accuracy of information within this publication but the publishers cannot be held responsible for any errors or omissions. Views expressed are those of the author and do not necessarily represent those of the publishers or the football club.

Photography © Arsenal Football Club.

Arsenal logo and crest are registered trademarks of The Arsenal Football Club plc.

ISBN: 978-1-907104-57-2

£7.99

CONTENTS

MANAGER'S MESSAGE

Dear Supporters,

Welcome to The Official Arsenal Annual 2011 - I hope you have an enjoyable read. There was certainly no shortage of excitement and promise during the 2009/10 season. As we have come to expect, the level of competition both domestically and in European competition was tough. We were unable to land a trophy during the season but I feel we took many positives and our young squad learned a great deal of valuable lessons.

All supporters will have their own special memories from an exciting campaign. From the early high-scoring victories against Everton and Blackburn Rovers, through the comebacks against numerous sides including Bolton Wanderers and Stoke City, to the final day when we confirmed our third-placed finish against Fulham - it was an action-packed League season. In Europe too we had many great ties including the 5-0 defeat of Porto and those dramatic ties against Barcelona.

I can assure you that everyone at Arsenal Football Club has prepared with thoroughness and excitement for the 2010/11 season. With our superb and ever-improving squad of fine players we know that we have every prospect of a successful and hopefully trophy-winning campaign. Of course, it is not just the players on the pitch and the coaching staff who make the Club what it is. Arsenal is a wonderful Club thanks too to you - the supporters. You are every bit as important as every other part of the operation and I thank you for your vocal and warm support. I can promise you that the players appreciate it too.

Here's to even better times ahead,

Arsène Wenger
Manager.

SEASON REVIEW

An exciting league campaign saw Arsenal often sitting where they belong - at the top of the table. Although the Gunners ultimately had to settle for third place it was a pulsating campaign full of drama. Here are the most memorable moments, month by month...

AUGUST

The Gunners began the season firing on all cylinders. New signing Thomas Vermaelen was among the goals at Goodison Park as Arsenal thumped Everton 6-1. Among the other goals was a 25-yard curler from Denilson and a counter-attack capped by a great strike from captain Fabregas. "We are top of the league," sang the jubilant travelling fans. Could they stay there?

The following Saturday they were in title-winning form again with a 4-1 victory over Portsmouth in the first home Premier League tie of the campaign. The win was spearheaded by two goals in four minutes from midfielder Abou Diaby. Another happy aspect of the tie was that it was Eduardo's first Premier League start since his horror injury at Birmingham City in February 2008.

The final league tie of the month was at Manchester United, the toughest challenge of the season to date. The hero against Portsmouth, Diaby accidentally put through his own net at Old Trafford. Wenger's team found it impossible to bounce back and despite a goal from Arshavin they notched up their first league defeat of the season.

15 August Everton 1-6 Arsenal
(Gallas, Vermaelen, Denilson, Fabregas 2, Eduardo)

22 August Arsenal 4-1 Portsmouth
(Gallas, Diaby 2, Ramsey)

29 August Manchester United 2-1 Arsenal
(Arshavin)

The Gunners began the season firing on all cylinders.

SEPTEMBER

The month of September would improve for the Gunners but it started as August had ended - with defeat in the city of Manchester. Arsenal faced two old boys in the shape of Emmanuel Adebayor and Kolo Toure but it was Manchester City who prevailed in a hard-fought match. Van Persie and Rosicky were on target for the visitors.

Back at Emirates Stadium the team bounced back in style with a 4-0 defeat of Wigan Athletic. Vermaelen had been named the player of the month for August by the Club website and he celebrated with two goals and a clean sheet. In securing the clean sheet he made a heroic close-range block in the dying seconds. Fabregas was also on the score-sheet.

Away to Fulham the following week it was Vito Mannone who was in heroic form. The goalkeeper pulled off a succession of spectacular saves to keep the Gunners in the London derby. Robin Van Persie scored in the 52nd minute and the team held onto his lead to finish the month on a high.

12 SEPTEMBER MANCHESTER CITY 4-2 ARSENAL
(Van Persie, Rosicky)

19 SEPTEMBER ARSENAL 4-0 WIGAN ATHLETIC
(Vermaelen 2, Eboue, Fabregas)

26 SEPTEMBER FULHAM 0-1 ARSENAL
(Van Persie)

OCTOBER

In the third minute of the clash with Blackburn Rovers the Gunners fell behind. However, in a season rich with comebacks the team went on to win 6-2. Goals from Vermaelen, Van Persie, Arshavin, Fabregas, Bendtner and Walcott completed a fine rout. The home fans were delighted by another high-scoring victory for their heroes.

The delight continued with a 3-1 victory over Birmingham City. The win was secured with goals by Robin Van Persie, Diaby and Arshavin. This tie was followed by a trip to West Ham United. It was a tough London derby and despite goals from Gallas and the in-form Van Persie the tie finished all-square at 2-2.

On the final day of the month came the first north London derby of the season. The match was enlivened by two goals in 60 seconds. Van Persie converted a cross from Sagna and straight from the restart the Dutchman fed Fabregas who scored the second goal. On 60 minutes Van Persie made it three, turning in another cross from Sagna. The Gunners had not heard the last of their local rivals though.

The home fans were delighted by another high-scoring victory for their heroes.

4 OCTOBER ARSENAL 6-2 BLACKBURN ROVERS
(Vermaelen, Fabregas, Arshavin, Van Persie, Walcott, Bendtner)

17 OCTOBER ARSENAL 3-1 BIRMINGHAM CITY
(Diaby, Van Persie, Arshavin)

25 OCTOBER WEST HAM UNITED 2-2 ARSENAL
(Gallas, Van Persie)

31 OCTOBER ARSENAL 3-0 TOTTENHAM HOTSPUR
(Fabregas, Van Persie 2)

NOVEMBER

Arsenal suffered from an own goal at Old Trafford in August but benefitted from two in one match in November. In their 13th successive unbeaten match at Wolves, Arshavin and Fabregas scored to take Arsenal to second place in the Premier League table.

It was a less happy affair a fortnight later when the Gunners travelled to the north-east to face Sunderland. Darren Bent smashed home with 19 minutes left to settle an even tie and consign Wenger's team to its third defeat of the campaign. Arshavin hit the side-netting but that had been as close as the visitors came to scoring.

By the end of the month the Club was in a difficult position in the title race, a full 11 points behind the leaders. The Gunners were on the wrong end of another own goal against Chelsea when Vermaelen put through his own net. Although Wenger's men had most of the possession they lost that tie 3-0. It had been an overall disappointing month in the league. December lay ahead with a busy fixture schedule...

7 NOVEMBER WOLVES 1-4 ARSENAL
(Fabregas, Arshavin)

21 NOVEMBER SUNDERLAND 1-0 ARSENAL

29 NOVEMBER ARSENAL 0-3 CHELSEA

5 DECEMBER ARSENAL 2-0 STOKE CITY
(Arshavin, Ramsey)

13 DECEMBER LIVERPOOL 1-2 ARSENAL
(Arshavin, og)

16 DECEMBER BURNLEY 1-1 ARSENAL
(Fabregas)

19 ARSENAL 3-0 HULL CITY
(Denilson, Eduardo, Diaby)

27 DECEMBER ARSENAL 3-0 ASTON VILLA
(Fabregas 2, Diaby)

30 DECEMBER PORTSMOUTH 1-4 ARSENAL
(og, Nasri, Ramsey, Song)

In the Club's 100th match at Emirates Stadium the Gunners were victorious.

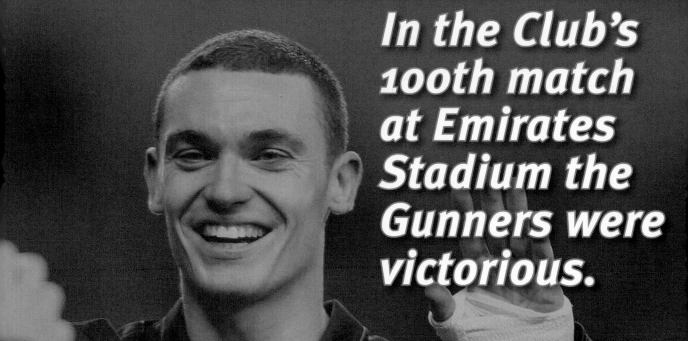

DECEMBER

In the Club's 100th match at Emirates Stadium the Gunners were victorious. Stoke City were the visitors and goals from Arshavin and substitute Ramsey saw them off. The next tie was at Anfield where Arshavin was on-target again as Arsenal went third with a 2-1 win.

At Burnley three days later Fabregas opened the scoring early but the goal was cancelled out by a penalty from Graham Alexander. With two more dropped points the Gunners would need to get back in their winning ways quickly - and they did.

Two successive matches either side of Christmas Day were both won 3-0 by Wenger's team. First they beat Hull City thanks in part to a fine free-kick from Brazilian Denilson. Their next victims were Aston Villa who were overcome with a brace of goals from Fabregas and one from his midfield ally Diaby. The final match of the month and of 2009 was at Portsmouth. The Gunners won 4-1 and the pick of the goals was a superb solo effort from Aaron Ramsey.

11

The win was especially pleasing because it took the Gunners back to the top of the table.

9 JANUARY ARSENAL 2-2 EVERTON
(og, Rosicky)

17 JANUARY BOLTON WANDERERS 0-2 ARSENAL
(Fabregas, Merida)

20 JANUARY ARSENAL 4-2 BOLTON WANDERERS
(Rosicky, Fabregas, Vermaelen, Arshavin)

27 JANUARY ASTON VILLA 0-0 ARSENAL

31 JANUARY ARSENAL 1-3 MANCHESTER UNITED
(Vermaelen)

JANUARY

On a freezing January day Everton visited the Emirates and nearly left with a warming win. Thanks to a last-minute strike from Rosicky the Gunners were able to salvage a point from the match. They then faced Bolton Wanderers twice in three days. The first was at the Reebok Stadium where the Gunners won 2-0.

Back at Emirates Stadium three days later Arsenal found it harder. They fell behind twice but pulled off another spectacular comeback with Fabregas and Arshavin among the goals. The win was especially pleasing because it took the Gunners back to the top of the table.

Sol Campbell re-signed for Arsenal in January and was thrown into the action at Villa Park, replacing the injured Vermaelen. He helped secure a clean sheet but Arsenal were unable to score, leaving the tie goalless. January ended with the chilling prospect of Manchester United. The recovered Vermaelen scored against United but by then the visitors had scored three times. Wenger's team did not want to lose to anyone, but this defeat was especially damaging to the title hopes.

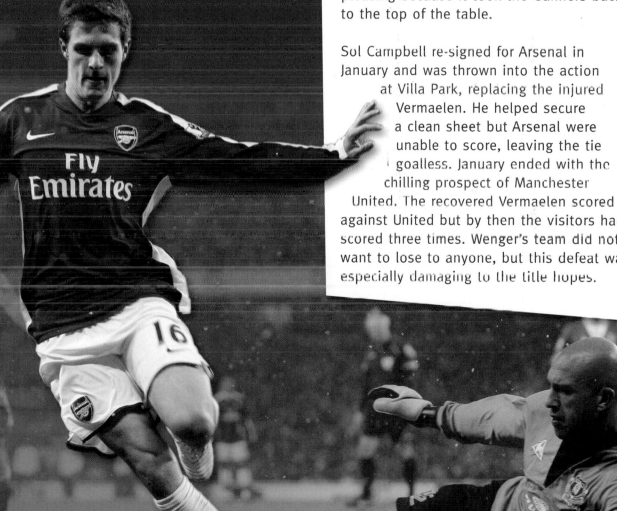

FEBRUARY

With Chelsea and Liverpool as their first two opponents of the month, Wenger's side would soon get a chance to put things right. Unfortunately, they lost the first tie with Chelsea's ever-lethal Didier Drogba scoring twice. A win against the Merseysiders was vital - and they got it.

With 18 minutes left, Tomas Rosicky sent in an inviting cross which Abou Diaby headed home at the far post. The home fans were in raptures and Arsenal were back in the title race - by their fingertips. It was also the 450th win of Arsène Wenger's glorious Arsenal reign.

Nicklas Bendtner had endured a mixed campaign so far but he opened the scoring against Sunderland. Arsenal's 2-0 win in that tie was confirmed with a late and successfully converted penalty from Cesc Fabregas. Could a late title charge be on the cards? When the Gunners swept aside Stoke City with a 3-1 win the month should have ended on a high. But a horrific injury to Aaron Ramsey, which left him with a double leg-break, cast a huge shadow over the renewed optimism.

7 FEBRUARY CHELSEA 2-0 ARSENAL

10 FEBRUARY ARSENAL 1-0 LIVERPOOL
(Diaby)

20 FEBRUARY ARSENAL 2-0 SUNDERLAND
(Bendtner, Fabregas)

27 FEBRUARY STOKE CITY 1-3 ARSENAL
(Bendtner, Fabregas(p), Vermaelen)

> *The home fans were in raptures and Arsenal were back in the title race - by their fingertips.*

MARCH

The month started well with a 3-1 win over Burnley at Emirates Stadium. Fabregas had opened the scoring on 34 minutes but hobbled off injured just minutes later. After Burnley equalised Walcott restored the Gunners' lead in style before Arshavin made the win safe at the death. At Hull City Walcott was in particularly creative form but it was Bendtner who was the hero, scoring the winner in injury time.

Back at Emirates, Wenger's team started well against West Ham United. Denilson opened the scoring in the fifth minute but a minute before the break the Gunners received a blow to their chances when Vermaelen was shown a red card. In the second-half the heroic 10-man home side did not only hold onto their lead but doubled it. Captain Fabregas struck home a penalty with just eight minutes left.

If the Gunners could claim three more points at Birmingham City in the final league tie of the month they would be in with a real hope of a tilt at the title come May. All seemed well when Samir Nasri fired home with just nine minutes left. The visiting fans were jubilant and confident. However, just as Arsenal had broken the hearts of opponents many times in the campaign with late goals, so did they face a taste of their own medicine. At the death Kevin Phillips slotted in an equaliser. It was a bitter note to end the month on.

6 March Arsenal 3-1 Burnley
(Fabregas, Walcott, Arshavin)

13 March Hull City 1-2 Arsenal
(Arshavin, Bendtner)

20 March Arsenal 2-0 West Ham United
(Denilson, Fabregas(p))

27 March Birmingham City 1-1 Arsenal
(Nasri)

SEASON REVIEW

APRIL

The Gunners were back on the happier side of the last-minute goal story in the first match of April. Deep into injury time at home to Wolves, Nicklas Bendtner headed home a Bacary Sagna cross to win the tie and send the home fans into wild celebrations. Next up was the north London derby - how the Gunners hoped for another win at White Hart Lane!

It was not to be. Bendtner again scored late on - in the 85th minute - but by that point Arsenal had already conceded two goals. It had been a tough night all round. After falling behind in the 10th minute the Gunners had received a second blow when Vermaelen hobbled off injured. With their prospects of a top-two finish ever dwindling, Arsenal needed to make no more mistakes for the remainder of the season.

By the 48th minute at Wigan the Gunners were 2-0 ahead - thanks to Walcott and Silvestre - and seemed on course for another fine away win. However, in the final 10 minutes of the match the home side stunned everyone by scoring three times and snatching victory away from Arsenal. The month ended with another disappointment - a 0-0 draw at home to Manchester City. The Gunners were out of the title race, but if they were not careful they would finish outside the top four.

APRIL 3 ARSENAL 1-0 WOLVES
(Bendtner)

APRIL 14 TOTTENHAM 2-1 ARSENAL
(Bendtner)

APRIL 18 WIGAN 3-2 ARSENAL
(Walcott, Silvestre)

APRIL 24 ARSENAL 0-0 MANCHESTER CITY

Wenger's team were back on sizzling form against the Cottagers.

"Cesc...

CESC FABREG...

"Cesc is a sol...
mate after thi...
Walcott who ...
The Gunners ...
Englishman a...
substitute wit...
With five min...
Gunners won ...
Fabregas was ...
heartbroken a...
card had rule...
the second-le...
Camp. He mad...
with the pena...
giving the gar...
the final five ...

MAY

With two matches remaining in the campaign the Gunners had a simple task on paper: win both of them and guarantee themselves a third-placed finish. However, on grass it was not to be as straightforward. Back in October the Gunners had thrashed Blackburn Rovers 6-2. In the return fixture at Ewood Park Van Persie gave the visitors a deserved early lead.

Just before the half-time break Dunn equalised for Rovers and then with 22 minutes remaining Blackburn took the lead. The Gunners kept pushing for another goal but it was not to be. Now, victory against Fulham in the final match of the season was imperative.

Having fallen away of late, Wenger's team were back on sizzling form against the Cottagers. Arshavin, Van Persie and Vela were all on target. A Fulham own goal made it 4-0 to the Gunners who secured a third-place finish. At the end of the tie the players made a lap of appreciation in front of their loyal fans. So many lessons had been learned during a challenging campaign. Here's to next time!

MAY 3 BLACKBURN ROVERS 2-1 ARSENAL
(Van Persie)

MAY 9 ARSENAL 4-0 FULHAM
(Arshavin. Van Persie, og, Vela)

L A

QUALIFYING ROUND

CELTIC V ARSENAL

18 August Celtic 0-2 Arsenal (Gallas, og)

A hectic first-leg at Parkhead was dominated by Arsenal who ran out deserved 2-0 winners. All the same, they needed a bit of luck to actually turn their domination into goals. Firstly, William Gallas deflected a Fabregas shot to take the lead before half-time. Then Celtic's Gary Caldwell accidentally converted a Gael Clichy cross past his own goalkeeper.

Euro Fact: Celtic had only lost once in eight European ties against English opposition at this ground.

EDUARD
16 SEPT
When the
respective
Arsenal w
of the sec
the match
last 11 mi
grab an u
After Verm
winner wa
minute. H
with his ki
strikes but

Nicklas
13 March
In the 14th
Arshavin po
fired the ba
Just 14 minu
again when
penalty spo
all-square b
minutes of i
of that perio
net to snatc

N
3
Ea
im
the
we
to
cel

ARSENAL V CELTIC

26 August Arsenal 3-1 Celtic,
(Eboue, Eduardo(p), Arshavin)

The Gunners were already in control of the tie and with the second-leg at Emirates they were confident of progression into the group stages. Goals from Eduardo, Eboue and Arshavin put the Gunners into a 5-0 aggregate lead before Celtic managed a last-minute consolation strike through Donati. By then Wenger's side was safely through and had maintained its status as very much a fixture in Europe's elite competition.

Euro fact: This game confirmed Arsenal's 12th consecutive season in the group stage of the Champions League.

GROUP STAGE

STANDARD LIEGE V ARSENAL
16 September Standard Liege 2-3 Arsenal (Vermaelen, Bendtner, Eduardo)

Two goals down in the first five minutes, away from home and in front of a hostile crowd. Who would have given the Gunners a chance of leaving Liege as winners? However, on his 100th Club appearance, Bendtner scored on the stroke of half-time. In the final 15 minutes of the tie the Gunners struck twice through Vermaelen and Eduardo. The hosts were stunned and Wenger's team were triumphant. What a sensational comeback!

EURO FACT: The last time the Gunners played in Liege they won 7-0!

ARSENAL V OLYMPIACOS
29 September Arsenal 2-0 Olympiacos (Arshavin, Van Persie)

For 78 frustrating minutes the Greek visitors managed to prevent the dominant Gunners from scoring. It seemed set to be one of those maddening nights when the ball simply refuses to cross the line. However, goals from Van Persie and then Arshavin gave the Club a deserved win. With two wins in their opening two ties the Gunners were already in control of Group H. There was an air of relief at the final whistle and also a hint of optimism.

EURO FACT: Nicklas Bendtner missed this tie after being involved in a minor car crash a few days previously.

AZ ALKMAAR V ARSENAL
20 October AZ Alkmaar 1-1 Arsenal (Fabregas)

The Gunners did not really have a goalscoring chance until nine minutes before half-time in this passionately contested tie. But when it came, they scored with it. Arshavin and Van Persie combined well to allow Fabregas to score at the far post. Arsenal would have deserved to win but in the third minute of injury time Mendes da Silva added a twist to the tale with an equaliser. All the same, this draw kept the Gunners at the top of the Group.

EURO FACT: This draw ended a run of Arsenal wins that had stretched for seven matches.

SEASON REVIEW

GROUP STAGE

ARSENAL V AZ ALKMAAR

4 November Arsenal 4-1 AZ Alkmaar (Diaby, Nasri, Fabregas 2)

Cesc Fabregas scored twice as Arsenal all but ensured qualification to the Champions League knockout stages with a 4-1 victory over the Dutch side. Nasri and Diaby were also on target as the Gunners managed to get the win that they had - in truth - deserved over in Holland. Jeremain Lens notched a consolation goal for the visitors in the 83rd minute but Arsenal had the points safe by then. They also had one foot in the knock-out stages thanks to their 10-point total.

Euro fact: Nasri's goal was his first since breaking his leg in pre-season.

ARSENAL V STANDARD LIEGE

24 November Arsenal 2-0 Standard Liege (Denilson, Nasri)

When Liege hosted the Gunners they scored twice only to see the visitors win the tie. In the return leg at Emirates Stadium the hosts scored twice and made sure they held onto the lead. Nasri and Denilson both scored in the final 10 minutes of the first-half to take control of the tie. However, in the opening 15 minutes the Gunners had spurned five clear-cut scoring chances so the story could easily have been different. By full-time Wenger's team were confirmed as winners of Group H. There was one more group tie to fulfil, then the knock-out stages beckoned.

Euro fact: Carlos Vela made his first start of the season in this tie.

OLYMPIACOS V ARSENAL

9 December Olympiacos 1-0 Arsenal

With the Gunners already confirmed as group winners this tie was quite naturally less intense than most. Wenger fielded a young side that included five teenagers and two debutants. The team could afford to lose and they did, after going behind two minutes into the second-half. However, the tie had given the mostly young team a wonderful experience of Champions League football. Once more, the fans and players alike could look with hope to the long-term future - and to the short-term future which began with a knockout tie against Porto!

Euro fact: The average age of the Arsenal line-up was 21.

By full-time Wenger's team were confirmed as winners of Group H.

GROUP STAGE

PORTO V ARSENAL
17 February Porto 2-1 Arsenal (Campbell)

The first knockout match for Arsenal was as hard-fought as you would expect - but also controversial too. The Gunners fell behind when Fabianski accidentally turned a Porto cross over his own line. However, within seven minutes they were level when Sol Campbell nodded in from close range. A free-kick was awarded against Arsenal in the second-half and was taken very quickly. The element of surprise took the team unawares and led to complaints the resultant goal should not have stood. Rosicky also had a good penalty claim dismissed. The 2-1 defeat left Arsenal with plenty to do in the return tie.

EURO FACT: This was Campbell's first Champions League game since the 2006 final v Barcelona. He scored then too!

ARSENAL V PORTO
9 March Arsenal 5-0 Porto (Bendtner 3[pen], Nasri, Eboue)

Nicklas Bendtner scored a glorious hat-trick as Arsenal reached the Champions League Quarter-Finals by overwhelming Porto 5-0 in the second-leg. Long gone were memories of the tense first-leg as the Gunners simply overwhelmed their opponents. Nasri and Eboue were also on target in the rout, but it was the Dane who the night belonged to. When he completed the hat-trick from the penalty spot in the final minute his joy was a wonder to behold. He was far from alone in feeling ecstatic - the Gunners were through to the quarter-finals!

EURO FACT: This was Bendtner's first Champions League hat-trick for the Club.

ARSENAL V BARCELONA
31 March Arsenal 2-2 Barcelona (Walcott, Fabregas [pen])

Nobody who witnessed this dramatic, action-packed tie will ever forget it. The audience were mystified that the first-half finished 0-0 after Barcelona had dominated proceedings - and in some style. Then when Ibrahimovic scored twice in the second-half it seemed Barcelona would get the win their dominance thus far deserved. Cometh the hour, cometh the young man - Walcott scored quickly after being sent on as a substitute. Then captain Fabregas netted a penalty at the end of the tie to grab a draw from the jaws of defeat.

EURO FACT: Due to a yellow card during this tie, Fabregas was ruled out of the return leg at his beloved Nou Camp.

BARCELONA V ARSENAL

6 APRIL FC BARCELONA 4-1 ARSENAL
(Bendtner)

In truth, it was always going to be an uphill battle for Arsenal to prevail. They were injury and suspension hit, Barcelona were on form, at home and with two precious away goals to their credit before a ball was kicked. Bendtner gave the visitors hope with a goal that capped fine work from Walcott. However, the talented Lionel Messi scored four on the night - including an impudent chip - to allow his side to sail into the semi-finals. The Gunners, meanwhile, were out. It had been a great campaign, but would not result in silverware.

EURO FACT: Former Arsenal captain Thierry Henry remained on Barcelona's bench

Bendtner's first Champions League hat-trick

THE SEASON IN PHOTOS

Relive memorable moments from 2009/10 with these stunning images of the action on and off the pitch.

Thomas Vermaelen signs for the Club, immediately strengthening the defence.

Denilson shoots and the first goal of the Premier League campaign is scored. The Gunners went on to win this tie against Everton 6-1.

Passion from Cesc Fabregas at Stoke City

Aaron Ramsey celebrates scoring the fourth Arsenal goal as the Gunners beat Portsmouth 4-1.

The dug-out celebrates Fabregas's goal against Spurs.

Sol Campbell returns to the Club.

The final goal of the season is scored by Carlos Vela against Fulham.

Theo Walcott ponders a tough match ahead at the Nou Camp against Barcelona.

A snowy day at Emirates Stadium in January.

CHAMAKH
29

New signing Marouane Chamakh joins the Club

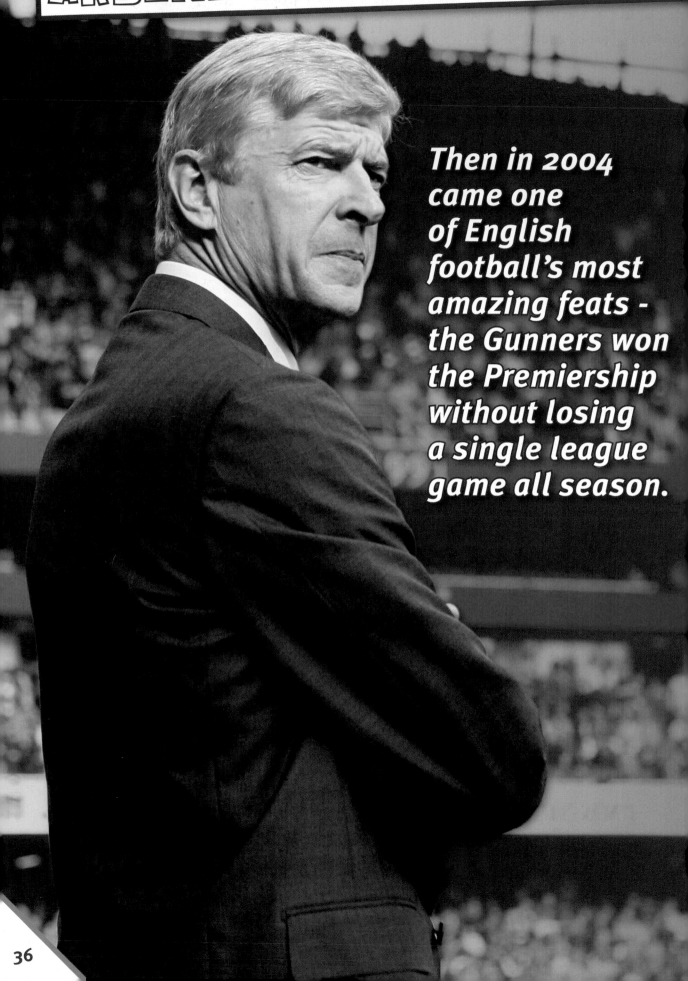

Then in 2004 came one of English football's most amazing feats - the Gunners won the Premiership without losing a single league game all season.

1996-2000: DAZZLING BEGINNINGS

Mr Wenger joined the Club in 1996. He immediately made a series of changes to the training regime and diets of the players. Some of his innovations have since been adopted by other clubs and national teams. During his first 10 months as Manager he bought new players including Patrick Vieira, Nicolas Anelka, Emmanuel Petit and Marc Overmars. The team played increasingly exciting and attractive football. In his first full season as Gunners boss Wenger guided the Club to the domestic double. The following season he came within a whisker of repeating this trophy haul: Arsenal reached the FA Cup semi-final and finished second in the Premier League.

2000-2002: DOUBLE DELIGHT AGAIN!

During these years Wenger continued to fine-tune the squad. New faces arrived including French striker Thierry Henry and attacking midfielder Robert Pires who between them gave the Gunners even more firepower. As Wenger regularly won Manager of the Month and other awards his stature in the game of football continued to soar. In 2002 the Club embarked on a phenomenal run of wins that culminated in another domestic double. The league half of this was secured with a 1-0 win at Old Trafford and the double was completed with a 2-0 victory over Chelsea in the FA Cup.

2003-2006: THE 49ERS

This period of his reign began with another FA Cup Final win - a Robert Pires goal was enough to sink Southampton. Then in 2004 came one of English football's most amazing feats - the Gunners won the Premiership without losing a single league game all season. Indeed, the Club continued the unbeaten run the following season eventually stretching it to a phenomenal 49 matches. In 2005 the Club won another FA Cup Final, overcoming Manchester United after a penalty shoot-out. The following season the Gunners reached their first Champions League Final. Reduced to 10-men in the first-half they were beaten 2-1 by Barcelona. Wenger was awarded an OBE from the Queen.

2006-NOW:

As the Club moved to its new home Wenger's influence was, as ever, pervasive. He played a key role in the planning of Emirates Stadium including the size of the pitch and the design and temperature of the dressing room. Arsenal now has a skilful young side that Wenger has painstakingly assembled from around the world. The Club is now a fixture in the UEFA Champions League and the team's style of play is arguably the most admired in the world of football. Arsenal regularly challenge for trophies on all fronts - with the genius Mr Wenger at the helm more silverware cannot be far away.

FACT FILE

Strasbourg, France, October 22, 1949

Mutzig, Mulhouse, Strasbourg

Strasbourg (youth), Cannes (assistant), Nancy, AS Monaco, Grampus Eight Nagoya

ARSENAL HONOURS:
Premier League Champions:
1998, 2002, 2004
FA Cup Winners:
1998, 2002, 2003, 2005
FA Charity/Community Shield:
1998, 1999, 2002, 2004
Manager of the Year:
1998, 2002, 2004
Honorary OBE: 2003

SEASON REVIEW

The Club again gave its younger players a chance to taste first-team action in the competition. They gave the supporters much to cheer about in the present and much to look forward to in the future. Here is the story of the 2009/10 Carling Cup Campaign...

ARSENAL v WEST BROMWICH ALBION

22 SEPTEMBER 2009 ARSENAL 2-0 WEST BROMWICH ALBION (Watt, Vela)

For the first 30 minutes of this the visitors were shading the play and looking good for a win. However, after they were reduced to 10 men after a sending off, they were quickly outclassed by the Gunners. On 68 minutes the visiting goalkeeper could only parry a shot which fell into the path of Sanchez Watt. He slotted home to cap a fine debut. A quarter of an hour from the end Mark Randall sent in a fine chip which hit the bar. Vela tucked away the rebound to double the lead. West Bromwich Albion were top of the Championship as this tie was contested, but it was the Gunners who came out on top in the Cup!

A quarter of an hour from the end Mark Randall sent in a fine chip which hit the bar. Vela tucked away the rebound to double the lead.

ARSENAL V LIVERPOOL

28 OCTOBER 2009 ARSENAL 2-1 LIVERPOOL (Bendtner, Watt)

The Gunners reached the quarter-finals of the Carling Cup for the seventh successive season with a fine home win over Liverpool. Both sides fielded relatively young sides so this was a great glimpse into the future of two of Europe's biggest clubs. Merida opened the scoring on 19 minutes with a fierce shot. Seven minutes later Liverpool equalised through Insua's dipping shot from 25 yards. This set up a tantalising second half which the Gunners prevailed in. Five minutes after the break Bendtner scored what turned out to be the winner, putting the crucial finishing touch to a slick move from Wenger's young side. There were plenty more chances for both sides in an action-packed tie, but the Gunners held on to win 2-1.

MANCHESTER CITY V ARSENAL

2 DECEMBER 2009 MANCHESTER CITY 3-0 ARSENAL

Arsène Wenger stuck with a mostly young side for this tie but the hosts opted for a more experienced line-up. Until the 50th minute the tie was goalless and reasonably even, but then Carlos Tevez put City 1-0 up with a shot fired into the top corner of the net. The Gunners did their best to maintain their poise but could do nothing to stop Wright-Phillips from doubling the lead with another stunning strike that sailed into the other corner of the net. City made it 3-0 when Vladimir Weiss netted at the death. Although City on balance deserved their win, the match was closer than the scoreline suggested. The young Gunners had impressed during the Carling Cup campaign, but here at the quarter-finals their involvement in the competition came to an end.

THE ARSENAL TRAINING CENTRE

Less than an hour's drive from Emirates Stadium is a venue just as important to the Club. The state-of-the-art Training Centre is where Arsenal's on-field excellence is planned and prepared for. Arsenal players from all levels use the facility, while at the weekend the Centre stages youth team matches as well as reserve team friendly matches. Here are the facts and figures of the Training Centre...

There are 10 full-size pitches. Three of these pitches are for the first-team, three are for the reserve team and three belong to the youth team.

So, what about the tenth pitch? This is where first team friendly matches and Under-18 league fixtures are played. It is named after the former Arsenal star and reserve team coach George Armstrong, who passed away in October 2000 after collapsing while coaching.

In the summer of 2007 an indoor pitch facility was also added to the Training Centre. The 70 metre x 50 metre pitch is used by players across the Club's setup.

Other facilities at the Training Centre include six changing rooms, a steam room, a swimming pool with adjustable floor, gymnasium, treatment rooms, massage baths, and a fine restaurant.

On average, 70 players use the Training Centre every day. International sides have occasionally used the facilities.

Between 1961 and 1996 the players trained at the former University College of London's site, which is a long goal-kick away from the current Training Centre. Manager Arsène Wenger was a key figure in the development of the present Training Centre. The contents and layout of the building were almost entirely decided by Arsène and his backroom staff.

The Training Centre hosts three full-time gardeners, 12 ground staff, four catering staff, three building supervisors, and the Manager's secretary and youth-team secretary.

In 2004 a dedicated press briefing building was opened at the site. This building, where the players and staff fulfil their media requirements, consists of 10 interview rooms and a press conference room, seating up to 100 people.

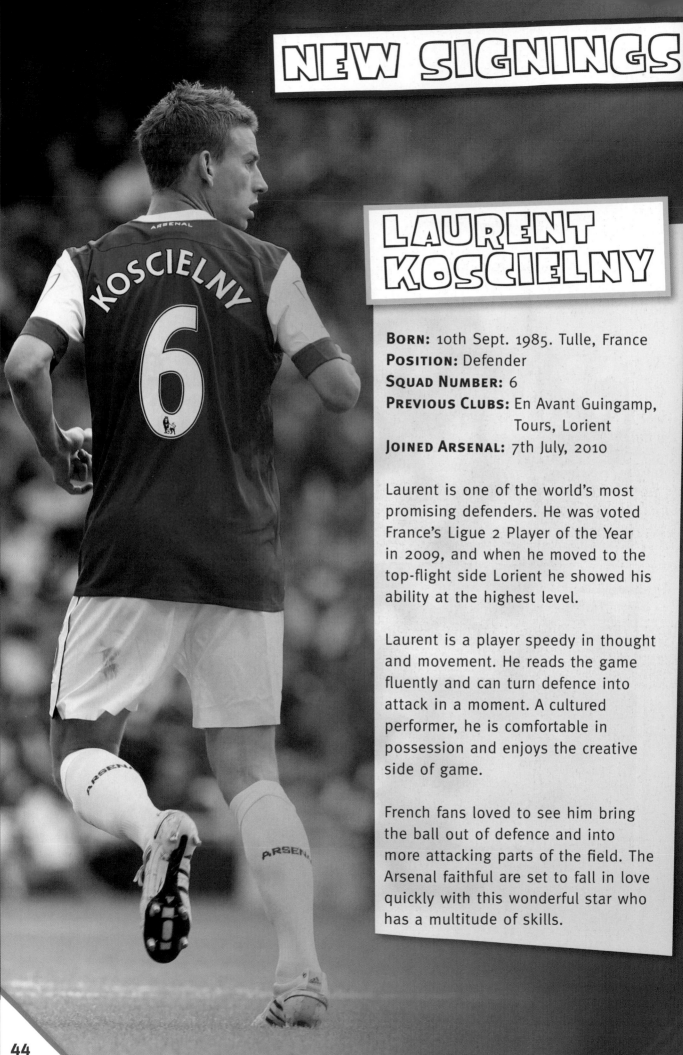

LAURENT KOSCIELNY

BORN: 10th Sept. 1985. Tulle, France
POSITION: Defender
SQUAD NUMBER: 6
PREVIOUS CLUBS: En Avant Guingamp, Tours, Lorient
JOINED ARSENAL: 7th July, 2010

Laurent is one of the world's most promising defenders. He was voted France's Ligue 2 Player of the Year in 2009, and when he moved to the top-flight side Lorient he showed his ability at the highest level.

Laurent is a player speedy in thought and movement. He reads the game fluently and can turn defence into attack in a moment. A cultured performer, he is comfortable in possession and enjoys the creative side of game.

French fans loved to see him bring the ball out of defence and into more attacking parts of the field. The Arsenal faithful are set to fall in love quickly with this wonderful star who has a multitude of skills.

MAROUANE CHAMAKH

BORN: 10th Jan. 1984. Tonneins, France
POSITION: Striker
SQUAD NUMBER: 29
PREVIOUS CLUB: Bordeaux
JOINED ARSENAL: 21st May, 2010

Arsène Wenger had coveted Marouane for some time before he finally secured the signature of the strike ace. No wonder the Manager was so keen: the Moroccan international is a phenomenal talent.

A strong man, Marouane was a key factor in taking his previous club Bordeaux to the French title and then assisting them during a fine run in the UEFA Champions League. He is fast, formidable and intelligent - all qualities that endeared him to Mr Wenger.

The hitman hit the ground running with the Gunners, with wonderful goal-scoring performances during pre-season. He was straight into the fray in the opening tie of the campaign against Liverpool, a key factor in the equalising goal. If he can continue to star in the Premiership and beyond, then the Gunners fans could be in for some magical, trophy-winning times.

GUNNERS TRIVIA QUIZ

STARTING AT THE BACK

1) What nationality is Lukasz Fabianski?
2) What year was Manuel Almunia born in - 1977 or 1987?
3) What is Gael Clichy's squad number?
4) With which team did Mikael Silvestre win the Premier League?
5) Which defender joined the Gunners for a second time during the 2009/10 season?
6) Which team did Thomas Vermaelen make his Premier League debut against?
7) And which team did he score twice against in September 2009?
8) What nationality is Kieran Gibbs?
9) Which Belgian side did Thomas Vermaelen score against in September 2009?
10) True or false: Vermaelen captained Ajax

MIDFIELD MAESTROS

1) What nationality is Denilson?
2) Which team did the Gunners sign Aaron Ramsey from?
3) Which Arsenal midfielder scored just 224 seconds into his Club debut in 2008?
4) How old was Jack Wilshere when he joined the Club: nine, or nineteen?
5) Which midfielder joined the Club from Zenit St Petersburg?
6) Is Tomas Rosicky Dutch or Czech?
7) Which Arsenal midfielder scored twice against Everton on the opening match of the 2009/10 season?
8) Who joined the Gunners from Bastia: Denilson or Alex Song?
9) Which former French Arsenal midfielder returned to face the Gunners with Manchester City?
10) Name the city and country in which Abou Diaby was born.

HOT SHOTS

1) Nicklas Bendtner scored a hat-trick against which Champions League opponents in March?
2) Which country does Robin Van Persie represent in international football?
3) Which opponents did Eduardo break his leg against in 2008?
4) Name the French side Marouane Chamakh joined the Club from.
5) Against which side did Nicklas Bendtner score a last-minute winner in April 2010?
6) Which side did Theo Walcott begin his football career with?
7) Name Arsenal's Mexican striker: Carlos _____
8) Which striker scored from the spot against Celtic in August 2009?
9) Who is the Club's all-time record goalscorer?
10) Robin Van Persie scored his first Arsenal goal against which team: Manchester City or Swansea?

CLUB HISTORY

1) In which year did the Club win the European Cup Winners' Cup?
2) And against which opponents did they win in that final?
3) Who was the first Club manager: Sam Hollis or Sam Nixon?
4) Who did Arsenal beat after a penalty shoot-out in the 2005 FA Cup Final?
5) Who was the Arsenal manager between 1986 and 1995, guiding the Club to numerous trophies including two league championships?
6) Name the first year the Club won the domestic double.
7) And in which other two years has Arsenal managed that feat?
8) Who did Arsenal beat in the 1987 League Cup Final?
9) True or false: when Arsenal won both domestic cups in 1993 this was the first time any club managed to do that.
10) In which year did the Club first win the league championship: 1931 or 1981?

THE MANAGER

1) True or false: Arsène Wenger played for Liverpool.
2) How many league titles has Mr Wenger won to date?
3) In which year did the Manager join the Club?
4) True or false: Thierry Henry was his first signing for the Club?
5) Which club did Mr Wenger join Arsenal from?
6) True or false: Mr Wenger's first opponents as Gunners manager were Cowdenbeath.
7) Which honour did Wenger receive in 2003: MBE or OBE?
8) Which team were the opponents for the first FA Cup Final of Mr Wenger's reign?
9) How many doubles has Mr Wenger won with Arsenal so far?
10) What is Mr Wenger's Assistant Manager called?

Answers on page 61.

WHERE'S GUNNER GONE?

Can you spot Gunnersaurus in the crowd?

KEEP THE FAITH 1987

VIVA CESC FABREGAS!

Arsenal.co

Australia   Arsenal.com/events

O2

JOIN Junior Arsenal® Gunners TODAY

✱Membership Pack ✱Exclusive Player Events
✱Chance to be a mascot ✱Chance to be a ballboy/girl
✱Access to reduced price match tickets (subject to availability)
✱Competitions ✱Newsletters

Junior® Gunners
Welcome to our World
✱0-3 years old

Junior® Gunners
Team JGs
✱4-11 years old

Junior® GUNNERS
Young Guns
✱12-16 years old

Available in all Arsenal Stores now
www.arsenal.com/juniorgunners
020 7619 5000

CHARTING THE PROGRESS

Here you can refer back to key milestones in the 2009/10 season and keep track of the equivalent moments in the 2010/11 campaign. Enjoy!

PREMIER LEAGUE	2009/10	2010/11
Final position	Third	
First home win	v Portsmouth 4-1	
First away win	v Everton 6-1	
First home draw	v Everton 2-2	
First home defeat	v Chelsea 0-3	
First away defeat	v Man Utd 1-2	

DOMESTIC CUPS	2009/10	2010/11
FA Cup	Fourth Round: Stoke City	
Carling Cup	Fifth Round: Manchester City	

CHAMPIONS LEAGUE	2009/10	2010/11
Progress	Quarter Final: Barcelona	
First home win	v Celtic 3-1	
First away win	v Celtic 2-0	
First home draw	v Barcelona 2-2	
First away draw	v AZ Alkmaar 1-1	
First home defeat	None	
First away defeat	v Olympiacos 0-1	

FIRST GOALS IN...	2009/10	2010/11
Premier League	Diaby v Portsmouth	
FA Cup	Ramsey v West Ham United	
Carling Cup	Watt v West Bromwich Albion	

THE ANSWERS!

CROSSWORD P.42

```
        B
M I D F I E L D E R S
    E   N         M
    N   D H I G H B U R Y        W
P   I   T   B A R C E L O N A    A
G O A L N   A       E            L
T   S   E   T   W   I            C
O   O   R U S S I A N            O
    N       E   L                T
  G U N N E R S E                T
  J         E                    
  U         H E N R Y            
  N                              
  I         F R E N C H          
P R E M I E R                    
```

SPOT THE BALL P.43

TRIVIA QUIZ P.54

STARTING AT THE BACK
1) Polish, 2) 1977, 3) 22, 4) Manchester United,
5) Sol Campbell, 6) Everton, 7) Wigan Athletic,
8) English, 9) Standard Liege, 10) True

MIDFIELD MASTERS
1) Brazilian, 2) Cardiff City, 3) Samir Nasri,
4) Nine, 5) Andrey Arshavin, 6) Czech,
7) Cesc Fabregas, 8) Alex Song,
9) Patrick Vieira, 10) Paris, France

THE HOTSHOTS
1) FC Porto, 2) Netherlands, 3) Birmingham City,
4) Bordeaux, 5) Wolves, 6) Southampton, 7) Vela,
8) Eduardo, 9) Thierry Henry, 10) Manchester City

CLUB HISTORY
1) 1994, 2) Parma, 3) Sam Hollis, 4) Manchester
City, 5) George Graham, 6) 1971, 7) 1998 and 2002,
8) Liverpool, 9) True, 10) 1931

THE MANAGER
1) False, 2) 3, 3) 1996, 4) False,
5) Grampus Eight, 6) False, 7) OBE,
8) Newcastle United, 9) Two, 10) Pat Rice

WHERE'S GUNNER GONE? P.56